# Martha's Mistake

Written by Poppy O'Neill

Illustrated by Esther Hernando

## Collins

Martha is drawing a picture of a dinosaur.
She chooses blue for the water and green for
the dinosaur's skin.

The jungle was green and lush

Oops! Martha has made a mistake. "Now my picture looks awful!" she thinks.

Martha scratches out her mistake, so no one will see that it's there.

But, it's no help. In fact, the mistake looks even bigger now. It's getting gigantic!

Martha keeps scratching. She hopes that will cover up her mistake but it just makes it look worse.

Martha sneaks a look at Paul's work.
Paul's looks wonderful! She wants her drawing to
match Paul's picture.

7

Martha feels awful. "What if Miss Palmer sees? She'll be angry. She'll tell Mum. She'll tell the head teacher!"

Martha wants to tear her picture in half and drop it on the floor. She wants to go home. She wants to scream!

Miss Palmer walks slowly around the classroom, helping children with their work. When she comes near, Martha leans across the desk to hide her mistake.

"Are you OK, Martha?" says Miss Palmer.

"I'm OK, Miss!" Martha tells Miss Palmer.

"Hide my picture, quick!" she whispers to Paul.

She hopes Miss Palmer won't see her picture.

"What did you give to Paul, Martha?" asks Miss Palmer.

"Nothing!" Martha yelps.

It isn't working. Miss Palmer has seen Martha's big mistake, which is now even bigger.

"I'm in big trouble," thinks Martha.

But Miss Palmer isn't angry.
"Nothing's wrong, Martha. Think about how you could turn your mistake into something else."

Martha feels confused. Miss Palmer makes it sound easy, but it's not!

Martha watches Miss Palmer write her poem. Oops!
She's made a mistake. Martha freezes – will
Miss Palmer be in trouble with the head teacher?

The jungle was green and lush
This dinosaur is not in a rush

But Miss Palmer leaves her mistake in her writing.
Then, she carefully adds some extra detail.

"That's it!" thinks Martha. She stares at her mistake. "How can I use my mistake to make my picture amazing, like Miss Palmer's poem?" she wonders.

Martha feels proud of her picture now.

"Look, Paul, my mistake is now another dinosaur, off on an adventure!"

Paul shares his picture with Martha. "Look," he points. Martha and Paul's pictures are matching after all!

# Martha's picture

# How to make your mistakes bigger and better

When you make a mistake, think about how you can learn something new. It could be a new animal for your picture!

A spelling mistake helps you remember next time.

# Mistakes help us learn

Mistakes help us learn lots better than getting it right first time. If you get lost, your walk takes longer. But you get to learn about new places and see new and interesting things.

Martha

In a similar way, making a mistake helps our brains learn new things.

school

29

# Martha's mistake

The jungle was green and lush
This dinosaur is not in a rush

# 🐾 Review: After reading 🐾

Use your assessment from hearing the children read to choose any GPCs, words or tricky words that need additional practice.

## Read 1: Decoding

- Point to the word **tear** on page 9. Say: This could be sounded out in two different ways – can you work out its sound and meaning by looking at the context? (**tear** /air/; means rip)
- Ask the children to read these words. Ask: Which two words do not contain the /air/ sound? (*near, learn*)

  **stares      near      carefully      learn      shares      there**
- Challenge the children to take turns to read a page aloud but sounding out words silently in their heads. Model reading a sentence aloud, fluently.

## Read 2: Prosody

- Model reading pages 14 and 15, demonstrating different voices for Miss Palmer and Martha.
- Say: To read their spoken words, we need to decide how these characters are feeling. As a group, discuss the characters' feelings.
- Encourage the children to read the dialogue with feeling, ensuring they read Miss Palmer's words as a question, and Martha's as an exclamation.

## Read 3: Comprehension

- Ask the children to describe any mistakes they have made, how they felt and what they did about them.
- Discuss what Martha learned in the story. If necessary reread pages 18 to 21, and draw out how mistakes are not bad, because we can learn from them.
- Ask questions about Martha's feelings, drawing on the children's own experiences.
  - On page 7, ask: What does Martha want? (*her picture to be like Paul's*) Have you ever felt like this?
  - On page 8, ask: Do you think the teacher will be angry? Why?
  - On page 9, Ask: Why does she want to scream? What would you say to her?
- Invite the children to retell the story in their own words, using the pictures on pages 30 and 31 as prompts.
- Bonus content: Challenge the children to summarise pages 26 to 29. Ask: How can mistakes be a good thing? (e.g. *you can: learn to draw a new animal; learn to spell a new word; find new places; discover interesting things*)